AMARANT

THE FLORA AND FAUNA OF ATLANTIS BY A LADY BOTANIST

COMPILED AND EDITED
BY

UNA WOODRUFF

G. P. Putnam's Sons
New York

Library of Congress Catalog Card Number 81-80622
ISBN 0-399-12625-2

Designed by Steve Henderson

Printed in Hong Kong

Acknowledgements
I would like to thank Christopher Blathwayt for his invaluable assistance
with translations, and also Hubert and Ines Schaafsma for their patience
and understanding throughout the production of this book.

U.W.

For Adam

Immortal Amarant, a Flour which once
In Paradise, fast by the Tree of Life
Began to bloom, but soon for Mans offence
To Heav'n remov'd where first it grew, there grows,
And flours aloft shading the Fount of Life,

Paradise Lost — Milton

Contents

Introduction

The curious drawings reproduced in this book have been taken from the notebooks of a seventeenth century artist, who specialised in botany, Lady Elizabeth Hurnshaw (1651-1703).

It appears, from the diaries which accompanied the drawings, that Lady Elizabeth set off to stay with relatives in America in 1681. She never arrived due to a remarkable incident but instead found herself on an island, which is to this day unmarked on the map. This island was called 'Amarantos' by the people who lived there but according to legend, even in Lady Elizabeth's time, it once,a long time ago had been called 'Atlantis'.

Lady Elizabeth spent nearly twenty years studying and drawing the strange flora of Amarantos. It was obvious that some great cosmic catastrophe in the past had caused the flora, and indeed, all vegetation on the island to mutate. This mutation had only beneficial effects on the Amarantines. They became total vegetarians and lived a life of peace unknown to the 'civilised world'.

Eventually Lady Elizabeth returned to England. She brought with her a collection of remarkable drawings and diaries.

In 1975, the antiquarian artist Una Woodruff found herself at Hurnshaw House. She met the last members of the family — the title had become extinct in the last century. The house itself, which must once have been so very beautiful and full of life, had disintegrated into a near-ruin. The family still remained there, but the windows were boarded up and the wooden beams would have cost nearly a million pounds to clear of death watch beetle. Burglars had helped themselves to the lead on the roof; it was not unusual to find a bucket in a top floor room under an open hole to the sky. The house had been neglected for so long; the family had become so decadent; the lack of both money and the will to succeed so consuming, that none of the surviving Hurnshaws had more than the vaguest idea as to what their house actually contained. Una Woodruff explored. And in the course of her explorations she found something that seemed to her, and the team of assistants working with her, the equivalent of Aladdin's cave. It was a library. George Hurnshaw, the present owner, knew nothing about it, except that there was a story in the family that many of the manuscripts, books, paintings and inscribed stone tablets, had come from the secret 'locked' library at Glastonbury Abbey. They had been sent to Hurnshaw House for safe-keeping at the time of the dissolution of the monasteries. George Hurnshaw was not a man who had concerned himself with books and he would have described the contents of the library as 'a load of old rubbish'. (Had he but known it, the contents of his forgotten library would have made him one of the richest men in the world, able to restore Hurnshaw House and twenty others besides.)

Una Woodruff has spent several years searching and cataloguing the Hurnshaw Library. There is much that she has yet to show the world of her findings.

Mortitia Adams, scientist and writer, joined Miss Woodruff in her work. Miss Adams is involved in research on the various forms of 'alternative' medicine which are at the moment so much in the public eye. She wanted to find out about the homoeopathic and healing qualities of the plants illustrated in 'Amarant'. Using Lady Elizabeth's diaries she was able to reproduce an account of what must have happened in the life of this strange and beautiful woman in the seventeenth century.

A Biography
of
Lady Elizabeth Hurnshaw

Lady Elizabeth was born in 1651, a last afterthought on the part of her parents. She was their seventh child, and her mother had also been born a seventh child. Elizabeth's Nanny used to tell her that the seventh of a seventh always inherited some special kind of awareness. The family lived in Cornwall; her father was Cornish by birth and her mother Irish. Elizabeth both inherited and lived with the great Celtic legends from her birth. Her nurse, well-known in the district as a 'natural' healer, taught Elizabeth the properties of the different plants she used medicinally. Elizabeth listened, and dreamed of a whole new world where health and life could be regulated by the simple application of the essence of flowers. The family Nanny's daughter, Martha, was the same age as Elizabeth, and when the latter met and married the young Sir Christopher Hurnshaw, Martha went too as Elizabeth's maid.

Christopher Hurnshaw was considered eccentric by his family.

The late seventeenth century was an era of port and horses, red-faced men and busty blonde women. Reading was not the done thing; hunting, shooting and fishing were. Christopher's father was horrified when he found that his son and heir refused to shoot even a rabbit. The boy said that he liked things living, not dead, and would eat nothing but vegetables. Christopher went further. He insisted on going to Oxford University to study science. Not even proper doctoring, his father would comment disgustedly over the third bottle of wine, where at least you learn something useful—such as chopping a man's leg off when he has got gangrene. Christopher learnt the science of botany. Edward Hurnshaw, Christopher's younger brother, realised at an early age that his father would have far preferred him to be the heir. His hopes began to rise when Christopher showed no signs of marrying.

Christopher Hurnshaw met Elizabeth when he was on one of his trips of exploration in Wessex. He used to go all over the country studying and collecting whatever rare botanical species he could find. As soon as Christopher saw Elizabeth, herself collecting wild flowers on a Cornish moor, he knew that this was the girl he would marry.

Elizabeth was lovely—but her looks were completely the opposite of the prevalent fashion at that time. She had long, straight black hair, green eyes from her mother, and all the ghostlike charm of the Celts. She was very thin, too; another point against her in her father-in-law's eyes. He liked women with great round bodies to indicate that babies would be no problem. The bigger the better was her father-in-law's view; and Elizabeth seemed to him insubstantial, as though she might vanish into the mist at any minute.

When seven years had gone by after their marriage, and Elizabeth had still failed to provide her husband with an heir to Hurnshaw, Christopher's father and his younger brother Edward grew more and more confident. They believed that this wisp of a girl would never have a child. They also thought that it was entirely her and her husband's fault for leading such unnatural and eccentric lives. The young couple never touched meat, never drank spirits, and never fought, either with each other or with other people. When attacked for their oddity, they both just smiled and replied calmly that it was their own life as they went on with their work. Sir Christopher became a founder member of the Royal Society, and a friend and contemporary of Sir Isaac Newton, Robert Boyle and the naturalist John Ray. His wife had always been a talented artist with an eye for scientific accuracy. Together they compiled many careful and detailed studies of botanical interest. Fragments of these have been found lately at Hurnshaw House, but they are too spoilt by time and neglect to restore. All the same, it is possible to deduce that the Hurnshaw's goal was to catalogue and categorise every known species of plant growing in England at that time. They went further. Rare and previously unknown specimens were brought back to Hurnshaw by travellers from the 'New World'. Heated glasshouses were built in the grounds of the estate that these exotic flora might survive. The Hurnshaws experimented in the hybridisation and propagation of their new acquisitions. It would seem that both had only the welfare of mankind, not its destruction, as their aim. Much of their work centred on the cultivation of plants which would provide good and healthy food. Famine was the great fear of that epoch; Christopher and Elizabeth felt that the answer lay in the ground around them and the vegetation which nature had provided.

The Hurnshaws discovered much, but they wanted more. For years they had been commissioning such seamen and travellers as they could contact to bring back specimens of vegetation from around the world. The method was not satisfactory. Those who are uninterested in plants take no care of them. Too often the cutting which could have been fascinating to the Hurnshaws arrived moribund and useless. It was, they decided, essential to go abroad and start finding out for themselves.

South America seemed a great deal further from England in the 1600's than it does today. The plans for the journey, the choice of equipment, took over a year to organise. The rest of the Hurnshaw family thought the couple were frankly mad to go junketing off across the seas just to pick up and preserve a few odd daisies and boil them up for tea, as Edward phrased it. Elizabeth and Christopher smiled again and took no notice. They had, moreover, a secret reason for happiness. Elizabeth was certain that she was at last going to have a child. And both wanted that child born away from the bucolic atmosphere of Hurnshaw House.

One week before they were due to sail, Christopher Hurnshaw was killed. He had gone riding, for pleasure and alone, to take a final look over the lands to which he was uncertain that he would ever return. His horse stumbled on a snare. Christopher was thrown against a wall and died within hours.

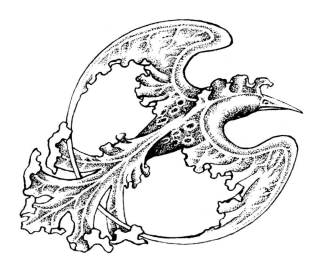

Elizabeth was so shattered by her husband's death that she just withdrew to her bed and stayed there. She was unable to think of the future. Elizabeth had not only been in love with Christopher; their work together symbolised all that she had ever wanted out of life. For many weeks she was as one dead and nothing could rouse her. It was a different kind of shock altogether which pulled Elizabeth out of this torpor. One spring evening she looked out of the window and saw the first snowdrops. It would be nice, she thought, to pick some for Christopher's grave. She got out of bed, dressed, and headed for the first time since her husband's death, for the open air. Elizabeth found that she could not get out. The door of her apartment was locked.

When Christopher died, Elizabeth had been in too great a state of apathy to object when her brother-in-law suggested that she move to the dowager's quarters in the house. Occasionally she heard his bucolic roars from the dining room and knew that he was getting drunk yet again on his brother's money. What she did not know was that he had proclaimed himself head of the family and Lord of the Manor. Nor did she know that he had dismissed herself from the scene by putting it around that she had gone mad from grief— and that anyway she had never been much better than a barren witch, playing with spells and calling it science. Nor did she know that her father-in-law was in league with Edward and backing him to the hilt. He had always found Elizabeth's interest in the arts both unhealthy and unfeminine; her failure to provide the House of Hurnshaw with heirs convinced him.

It was her maid Martha who told Elizabeth the truth. Edward, who was married by now, and already had two sons of his own, got drunk one night and shouted out that if that black witch Elizabeth thought the baby she was carrying was ever going to inherit Hurnshaw she could think again. If nature didn't see to it arriving in this world still born, he would. *His* son was going to get the lot, not some brat that played with flowers.

Martha overheard and told her mistress.

Anger had never been a part of Elizabeth's character until she heard this bit of news. It became so. Elizabeth would not fight for herself, but she would most certainly fight for her child. She was no fool. Elizabeth knew just how high the infant mortality rate was in the seventeenth century in Britain. This was one of the projects with which she and her husband had most concerned themselves. Her baby was already showing signs of its existence within her. Elizabeth knew that the time had come to move.

The escape, for such it had to be, was relatively easy. There remained many servants at Hurnshaw who had loved the gentle and courteous way of life that Sir Christopher had inaugurated—and who resented his bullying brother. When they were told by Martha that Elizabeth was expecting a child, who even if born far away, would one day return to Hurnshaw, they helped. Fear, particularly fear for the safety of an unborn child, induces cunning. Elizabeth wrote out the facts of her life to date before she left. She wrote that she just knew that the baby she was bearing would be a boy and not a girl, and that he would be the rightful heir to the estate. She hid this document in the Library. In it she adds that she is going to Virginia, in North America, where many of her own family had recently settled, until the boy should come of age and that then she would bring him back to claim his own estate.

In the spring of 1681, Lady Elizabeth Hurnshaw and Martha set off.

The Hurnshaw family was to hear no more of Lady Elizabeth for some eighteen months. Edward settled down to the serious business of gambling away the family assets. His sons grew up in his mould. Their mother died quietly; no doubt from exhaustion, after giving birth to yet another red-faced replica of his father. The family had almost begun to convince themselves that Elizabeth had gone out of their lives for good and all when Martha turned up one night at the manor. She was exhausted but coherent, and the story she had to tell set Edward drinking with joy.

Martha reported that she and Elizabeth had arrived safely in Virginia. There they rested, and Elizabeth gave birth to a son, whom she named Adam. Elizabeth had managed to contact her relations. It transpired that they had gone to America to avoid persecution in Cornwall because they belonged to a heretical religious sect known as the 'Uranteans'. These relatives were now leading a new and happy life in the country some distance to the west of Virginia. Elizabeth and her son were to come to them at once. But they were to take great care on their journey, because it would be necessary to pass through Indian territory on the way to their settlement. The attacks on white travellers had become only too well-known in that part of America.

And that was precisely what did happen to Lady Elizabeth and her group. They were attacked by Indians one night along their way. Lady Elizabeth refused to shoot because it was against her principles to kill. Martha, herself, had run away and hidden in a hut behind the house where they had been staying the night. When the trouble had died down and the yelling Indians had gone, Martha came out. She found the house razed to the ground. There was no sign of Lady Elizabeth or the baby. Everything had been burnt. Martha lay low in the hut for some weeks hoping for news of her mistress, but eventually came to the conclusion that there neither would be nor could be tidings of her ever again. Elizabeth must either have been trapped in the fire and died, or been carried away by the Indians — in which case she certainly would never be seen alive again. Martha struggled back to England, working her passage across the ocean as a maid to a gentlewoman, and eventually back to Hurnshaw House because she felt it her duty to tell Edward what had happened.

It is unnecessary to say that Edward Hurnshaw and his sons not only accepted this tale without a murmur, but also with great relief. Martha was reinstated at the manor and lived on with the memories of what-might-have-been for another thirty four years.

Lady Elizabeth faded from the Hurnshaws' lives for nineteen years. If Edward and his sons remembered her at all, it was only as a tiresome problem of the past, from which they had quite rightly been delivered by a most discerning Fate. Edward became a grandfather; the succession was secure. Life in the manor carried on in Edward's way, the way of the drinking, sporting, upper classes in England at the end of the seventeenth century. Learning and science were at a premium. Money belonged to those who had it. The peasants who would not pay their rent were evicted and starved (or hung for sheep-stealing); but their overlords lived on in pleasure.

Christopher Hurnshaw's heated glasshouses fell down and were not replaced. The herb gardens that he and Elizabeth had cultivated so carefully went to seed. There remained one or two old people in the village whom Elizabeth had been trying to teach in her own way the craft of healing through the medium of plants. Such people carried on what they had learnt in secret. Edward Hurnshaw, had he discovered them, would certainly have had them branded and punished as witches.

Edward was to find, however, that this halcyon period of his life was based on a false premise.

He did not know that thousands of miles away, off the African gold coast, a British ship had recently rescued two strange white people. One was a woman, the other a young man. The woman clutched a wooden casket, which never left her or her companion's sight. She seemed to be in command of the young man, and said that she came from a great English artistocratic family. The seamen, assuming that they had been ship-wrecked, took them aboard. Their appearance, after what transpired to be weeks of living in the jungle of Africa, was surprising. They seemed healthy and mentally alert. The woman explained that this was because they had been living entirely on a diet of the local vegetation. The seamen were impressed; until the lady tried to tell the story of how they came to be wandering alone in Africa. It was not possible for ordinary British seamen to accept the tale she spun. Privately they decided that she was talking nonsense and had gone mad as a result of unmentionable horrors. However, the couple behaved quietly and seemed harmless, so the Captain of the ship left them in peace and brought them home to England.

In the summer of 1702, the Captain of this ship arrived at Hurnshaw House and announced that he had brought back the Lady Elizabeth. He hoped for a reward; Edward nearly set the dogs on him. At that moment Elizabeth walked in.

There could be no doubt. Edward, Martha and many of the other people in the manor who had known her long ago saw the same Lady Elizabeth that they had always seen. Her appearance had not changed at all. She had not aged in any way whatsoever. Her face and figure were still those of a woman in her early thirties. The skin had no wrinkles. The hair was exactly the same natural black. The eyes, to those like Martha who noticed, were possibly different. They seemed lighter and more ethereal than ever.

Edward's first thought was that he really must cut down on the mead; he had started seeing things. His second, when the whole household had recognised—and welcomed—her, was that it was going to be difficult to get rid of his sister-in-law. Too many people had been present when the ship's captain brought her in for the obvious solution to be anything but suspect.

Elizabeth had taken precautions; she knew very well that Edward's first reaction to her reappearance would be to try and eliminate her. So she left Adam, with the casket and her notebooks and diaries, at an inn before tackling Hurnshaw House. He had instructions as to what to do if she did not get in touch with him. Elizabeth's security was in her son, and she knew it.

Edward, when he heard what she had to say, and knew that Adam was waiting at a secret address, had a stroke. It left him with one side of his face paralysed.

Before she sent for her son, Elizabeth insisted that the whole Hurnshaw family should listen to her account of all that had happened since she went away. She told them that she had proof, in her drawings and diaries, and above all, in the existence of her son—who had not attained 'immortality', as yet—and would arrive as a completely normal boy of twenty one to prove the truth of his mother's story. But not, said Elizabeth, until you accept me and him as what we are; the rightful owners of Hurnshaw House and all that is left of its estate. Edward listened.

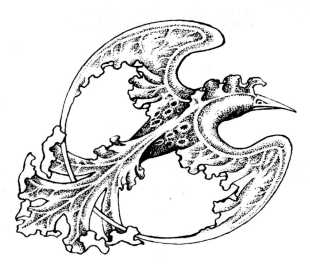

Elizabeth began by explaining why she seemed not to have aged. She had drunk of the essence of a plant which makes it possible for human beings to transcend time. She had found this plant at the centre of a maze on an unknown island named Amarantos after the beautiful, indigenous flower called the Amarant, which also provides the guide to the 'Flower of Immortality' hidden in the maze. Elizabeth explained that it was not yet clear how long the effects of this magical plant would last; she did not know whether she had achieved true immortality or whether time would catch up with her in the end. Few people even among the Amarantines had ever discovered the Flower but all knew of its existence right in the centre of their land. Elizabeth had found it in the course of an adventure that she could not rationalise, but which the Hurnshaws would just have to accept.

When the Indians attacked the settlement in America on her journey to join her cousins, Martha escaped by hiding in a hut. Lady Elizabeth, carrying her baby son, refused to shoot on principle, but managed to slip away through the fires and the yelling Indians to a nearby river. She felt some power must be guiding her to sanctuary, and followed her instinct without question. At the edge of the river she found a small boat waiting, empty but for its oars. Elizabeth paddled downstream, but eventually fell asleep, cradling her baby in her arms. When she woke up she was frightened to find that one of the oars had been lost overboard, and the boat was drifting through an estuary out to the open sea.

For a day they drifted further and further into the ocean. And then, as if from nowhere, a curious ship came across the flat blue sea and drew up alongside her. This ship was unlike anything she had ever seen. It was made of bright metal, and seemed to glide over the waves without touching them. There were neither oars nor sails but it moved with the speed of a bird.

The crew's appearance was strange as well. They all had skins so fair that they seemed translucent. Everything about them seemed to radiate sun — their hair, and their clothes, and their manners as they helped Elizabeth and the baby on board, shone with brightness and courtesy. They looked like young Greek gods, and the language they spoke seemed to Elizabeth to resemble ancient Greek. The ship and its passengers glided away in the direction of the sun, and came to a stop on an island. At first Elizabeth tried to work out where she was; could it be South America? Later she stopped bothering and was content to be in the most beautiful place that she had ever imagined.

Elizabeth and the baby began life on Amarantos staying as guests of an elderly couple.

The house she was taken to was again unlike anything Elizabeth had ever met. The architecture had the lightness of a Greek temple and the mystery of a mediaeval or Gothic castle. Inside everyone lived on the floors, but in great comfort. The beds were on the floor, made of soft rushes, and the pillows were constructed from petals. Their first meal was the most delicious Elizabeth had ever known. She was told that the food came entirely from plants and the mellow drink from the dragon vine which covered the walls of the house. They went out and the landscape and the gardens were even more remarkable than the house. It was obvious that the old couple dedicated their days to their gardens. Everything was looked after with meticulous care. The plants, again totally unknown to Elizabeth, were particularly strange. It seemed that many of them, instead of bearing flowers, gave rise to brightly coloured butterflies, humming birds, lizards and other creatures she did not recognise. Elizabeth realised that it was these fruitful plants which had been providing the music she had heard around her ever since she landed on Amarantos.

Elizabeth went straight to work studying these extraordinary plants, happy for the first time since her husband's death. Sometimes she became sad again, thinking how much Christopher would have loved to share her discovery, but common sense told her that the next best thing to having him with her, was to get on with what they had always dreamt of doing even if she had to do it alone. She drew all she saw. She made notes on the properties of each plant and tapped the knowledge of her host and hostess. They knew much about the nutritional and healing powers of each one already, but they were impressed by her interest and understanding of botany. Adam grew up as strong and fair as the children he played with on the island. Elizabeth told him his history, and explained as soon as he was old enough to understand that he was different from the Amarantines. She taught him English and what she knew of European history. She explained the difference in attitudes and cultures between the world they had left and the world they had found. For she never lost faith that one day he would return to Hurnshaw. There was no reason why son should not have the benefit of both worlds—and to bring together the best of both. Her most difficult job was to explain to him the concept of crime. There was no such thing in Amarantos; nor malice, envy, corruption and hate. People lived in peace. There was enough land to go round amongst the small population. The land provided enough to live on. The need for power struggles did not arise.

Elizabeth was told that the most respected body of people in the country were known as the 'Royal Society of Botanists'. These people had spent their lives working along the same lines as Elizabeth and Christopher Hurnshaw. They experimented and catalogued the various properties of the plants on the island.

Eventually they heard of Elizabeth, and of the way that she, too, was both interested and very well-informed in botany. An invitation was sent to her to join them. This, she was told by her host and hostess was the highest honour that could be given in Amarantos.

Elizabeth and Adam were escorted to the headquarters of the Royal Society. These were in the grounds of the King's Palace. The gardens surrounding the compound were enormous. Apart from the Palace itself, a shining white building, with lapis lazuli domes and gilt stuccoes, there were temples and shrines and many strange buildings where the Royal Society cultivated their seedlings and carried out their tests. In the middle of the estate was a vast maze, a mile square. It was at the centre of this maze, Elizabeth learnt that the most sacred plant of all was to be found. She learnt as well that the only clue to guide one through the maze was to be found in the Amarant flower. The flower itself is made up of two dormant butterflies. When two lovers meet and hold the blossom of the Amarant, once in a million times the two parts of the flower will separate and transform themselves into butterflies. This, and only this, is the sign that the love between the two people is eternal and true. The butterflies lead the couple to the centre of the maze, and there they find the one plant that can transcend time. Love of the absolute kind can live forever. Of course every young couple who thought themselves in love tested the Amarant. It had been a long time since anyone had passed successfully.

Elizabeth and Adam were given a small house in the gardens of the

Palace, and she became one of the team involved in drawing all the plants for the great survey that the Royal Society had been working on for fifty years

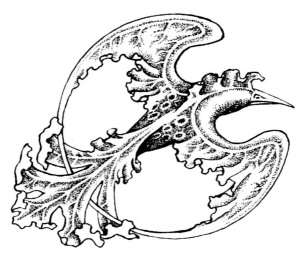

The years went by calmly and productively.

The Royal Society told Elizabeth the history of the island and its inhabitants.

The present name of 'Amarantos' or 'Amarant' had been used since the history of this island came to be recorded. But legend had it that many centuries ago the name had been 'Atlea' or 'Atlantis'. The current belief was that in those days the people of the island had achieved an extraordinarily high level of civilisation. They had been self-sufficient and lived in harmony. But, as with all such golden eras, time had corrupted the people. The results had been wars, erosion of the land, and in the end, volcanic eruptions followed by floods. The island had nearly sunk beneath the sea. Only a few of its population had survived. They understood, seeing the wreckage of their once lovely land, that nature intended them to rebuild a civilisation on the principles of the original inhabitants. Their leader impressed upon those who remained that they would have to go back to the basics of life if they were to recreate its ease. He was a distant ancestor of the present leader, King Eunor. He drew up a constitution. It meant freedom to live in peace, and self-sufficiency from the earth. Those who had survived the catastrophes of nature had in themselves changed. They wanted no more of the horrors they had just escaped. Amarantos was born again as a working Utopia.

In time, the Amarantines reclaimed their land from the sea. They built dykes, and lands which had been submerged rose again and were cultivated once more. It was found that the natural life of the island had also changed in some curious way. The vegetation which began to grow seemed to have a life of its own. Some of the plants and trees produced insects, birds and animals instead of fruit and flowers. Others continued to bear the essences of vegetarian living. The Royal Society of Botanists was established. Its job was to correct the balance of all wild life and natural growth on the island. They advised the farmers which crops to cultivate and the women which plants to distil or to cook. They experimented with propagation, and produced yet further improvements. The island prospered, and the people with it. They grew fair and strong and with no concept of corruption.

The Royal Society was more than a purely scientific group to the Amarantines. If a worship of botany was the 'religion' of the island, the members of the Society were its high priests. They were goverened by a strict code of morals and manners, and travelled all over the island visiting their people. Anyone could come to them for advice and no payment was ever expected. Indeed money did not exist on Amarantos. There was a system of barter, and if there should be any doubt as to the relative value of the goods exchanged the member of the Society would arbitrate. Thus Elizabeth found herself living among people who were both judge and jury, government and cardinal.

In time, she was made a member of the Society. Then, at last, she was told all the secrets of their culture. She learnt about 'The Flower of Immortality'. In the centre of the great Palace maze there was a pool. Under its water grew a strange white thorny plant. The Society believed that this had been thrown up from the sea during the dark ages. Very few had ever reached the centre of the maze and partaken of the flower, but to those that had was given the gift of eternal youth. This thorny white flower was the emblem of the Royal Society; it was the greatest ambition of everyone on the island to find it. The Society considered that the reason for the translucent quality of the Amarantines' skin came from this flower. Whoever became immortal naturally outlived many wives or husbands; their children on one side at least inherited the glow of youth.

The King of Amarantos, Eunor, had commissioned the Society to prepare a great survey of the island. Elizabeth was detailed to illustrate it. The book was bound in gold and set with the brightest jewels and lapis lazuli. Elizabeth felt immensely honoured. She did some of her finest painting at this period, and the Royal Society were delighted. Finally, the book was finished. Elizabeth was invited to the Palace to be presented to the King.

Elizabeth had heard much about King Eunor. She knew that although his mother was one of the immortals, he had not, as yet, himself found the way to the centre of the maze. He had not married, because he said that one day he would meet a woman who would lead him there, and until then he would remain single.

As soon as they met, King Eunor knew that that woman was Lady Elizabeth. It was irrelevant that she came from a different world. Together they would make a new world that joined the best of hers and the best of his. But, like all the men Elizabeth had ever known, he was cautious of committing himself. He would not marry her until he was certain that their love was real.

King Eunor shilly-shallied for a year before putting their love to the ultimate test — the Amarant flower.

One early summer morning, he asked her to try the Amarant with him. Trying the flower was the equivalent of a proposal of marriage on Amarantos. The only difference was that the flower decided, rather than the people themselves, what the answer should be. Naturally many Amarantines had gone against the flower's decision; but the King took the view that he would be dishonest if he didn't personally abide by the island's historical test. Much as he loved Elizabeth, she would have to go if the flower said "No" and failed to separate into two butterflies.

Neither wanted anyone to watch while they tried the test. In the past, King Eunor had tried it with three or four other ladies in front of witnesses, and each time it had been a failure. This time he was going to change the pattern.

Elizabeth and the King joined their hands round the stem of the most luscious blossom of the Amarant in the Palace gardens and waited. Slowly the flowers began to sway. It seemed to become alive. The petals moved. Their colour changed. Blue became white; the petals became wings. Two glorious butterflies shook themselves as though from a long sleep, and settled on the King and Elizabeth's hands.

The two smiled at each other triumphantly, and then they both felt as though the butterflies were pulling their hands. The King told Elizabeth they must follow where they were led. They were steered to the centre of the maze, found the pool, and the white thorny plant, drank its juices, and returned to the Palace to announce that they would be married immediately.

Adam was five years old when his mother married the King. He had never known his own father, and the King had never had any children. They took to each other straight away. Elizabeth soon gave birth to a baby girl, and then, two years later to another one. The family had become complete. Adam had been indoctrinated since his birth that he was different from his sisters, but he never really believed it. The Jesuits say 'Give me a child until it is seven'; Amarant had been Adam's home for far longer than seven years when the time came for Elizabeth to broach the subject of her return to England so that her son might claim his own estate.

The King agreed at once. He agreed because he was an honourable man and he knew that Adam must be given the right to choose. But he made it quite clear to Elizabeth that his hope was that Adam would reject Hurnshaw and all it entailed, and decide of his own volition to return to the island. Should that happen King Eunor told Elizabeth, Adam would be proclaimed his heir. They had had no sons of their own; the young Princesses would marry and lead their own lives. The King wanted Adam to return as much as he wanted his wife to, but he would exert no pressure on either. He would know, he told her, whether they wished to stay in England or come back to him. And if it were the latter, he would arrange things. He never explained how, but then he never explained anything. He was the kind of man who believed in 'living into the answer'. She felt that he was taking their departure rather too calmly, but he reminded her of the time some fifteen years before when they had found the centre of the maze together and she was reassured. She had agreed that her absence would be for no more than a year, and the length of Adam's would be up to him. The King reasoned what was the point of worrying about one year apart when they had the whole of time ahead of them.

Elizabeth and Adam were seen off by the King from Amarantos. He refused to tell her of the plans he had made to get her to Hurnshaw. There were many things that Elizabeth had as yet to learn for herself about the powers of the Amarantines. They set off in one of the golden flying ships, such as that in which they had first been rescued, and glided quietly over the water for many hours. Then something happened. Neither Elizabeth nor Adam could rationalise it. The sky went black; the ship just disappeared; they found themselves sitting on a white beach at the edge of some unknown sea. Elizabeth had packed clothes and beautiful presents to take to her son's family. She wanted Edward to receive him kindly. But everything had gone. She found the only object left to her was a small wooden casket filled with the notes and paintings she had made on the island. They had no idea what would happen to them next. The only thing they were sure of was that they would survive.

Adam found that the land behind the beach was full of edible vegetation. They lived on spring water and green plants and fruit for days that they ceased to count. Elizabeth passed the time telling her son as much as she possibly could remember about the life she had once lived at Hurnshaw.

Eventually they were rescued by the British ship and taken to England.

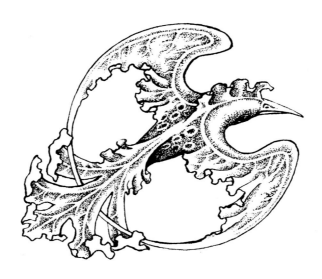

Elizabeth finished her story by adding that it was irrelevant whether they believed her or not. She had arranged with her son that if he heard no word of her within twenty four hours, he was to go straight to the Courts and make legal application to be recognised as the rightful owner of Hurnshaw.

Edward knew that he had to give in. He would, or his son would, find a way to get rid of these lunatics later. Adam was sent for and it was obvious to all who saw him that there could be no doubt as to his parentage. He had his father's voice and gestures, his mother's looks. Edward suffered another stroke, which left him incapable ofspeech.

And so Adam and his mother took over the reins of the Hurnshaw estate. They started as they meant to go on, with their minds full of love and goodwill. Adam rebuilt the glasshouses and restored the gardens. Elizabeth began a school to teach the tenants the science of botany. But their audience was unreceptive. Some of the old people, who remembered the happy days when Elizabeth and Christopher had managed the estate, welcomed their son and followed his ideas. But the younger generation, those who had grown up in Edward's time, thought very differently. Edward's son spread propaganda throughout the villages. He circulated the belief that both mother and son had gone insane as a result of their years of wandering homeless across the world. The villagers believed him. One day there was an incident of unparalleled horror in Adam's life. His mother, while drawing peacefully in the woods, was attacked by a mob of louts from the village. They threw stones at her and called her a witch. Luckily she was rescued. But after that, Adam asked his mother to stay within the manor grounds.

This state of affairs went from bad to worse. After only a few months, Adam and Elizabeth found themselves virtually prisoners in their own house. Once again the vandals crept back into power. Edward's son gloated and waited. He knew it would not now be long before the local people did for him that which he could not do without their support. A campaign of arson began. First the greenhouses were burnt; then the distilleries. A petition was sent by the villagers to the local magistrate, asking for Adam and his mother's conviction as sorcerers. When an epidemic disease broke out in the neighbourhood people burnt effigies of Elizabeth and Adam in public. These two did nothing to retaliate and this, to people who were used to a life of aggression, indicated evidence of their guilt. They could not know that Elizabeth and Adam spent night after night wondering how they could get back to Amarantos.

Elizabeth's mind was easy now. She had offered to her son the world that was his birthright, and he had rejected it. The King had been shrewd in suggesting that the boy must be given the chance to choose for himself, and right when he added that he was not worried about the outcome of that choice. Amarantos would regain its natural heir, though Hurnshaw would lose theirs.

It was the question of timing that frightened Elizabeth. By the end of the summer she was living in a state of siege. In the darker moments of the night, Elizabeth lost faith and felt that both she and her son would be killed before the King came.

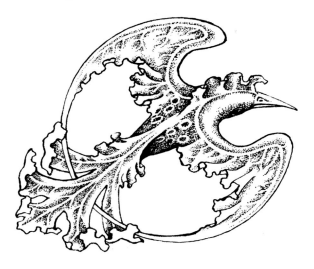

Elizabeth and Adam's final departure from Hurnshaw House took place in the autumn of 1703. No-one has ever been able to explain in terms of logic how they finally left. But there are legends still alive in the family and the villages around the manor. There is a certain upstairs window which is said to be the last place where they were seen. The story that they were spirited away by a creature from another world lent credence only to the prevalent belief that both were in league with the devil.

During the recent research into her remarkable life story a strange piece of new evidence came to light. Lady Elizabeth had taught her maid Martha to read and write, and encouraged her to keep a diary. A single page of this diary was found hidden in the spine of one of Elizabeth's notebooks. It was clearly written by Martha herself, for the spelling and grammar were not those of an educated person. It would seem that the maid was a witness to Elizabeth and Adam's inexplicable disappearance. She wrote:—

"On the twentieth day of September (1703) a stranger came to the house to enquire of her Ladyship. He were noble in stature with fair complexion and his dress were the queerest I did see even in the Amerikas. He wore a suit which closely covered his whole bodye save his head which were bare. The cloth were bright silver in hue and shone as it were touched by light. The master (presumably Edward's son) gave out that her Ladyeship were not at home and gave orders so the dogs were unleashed. But the man said he would call again on the morrow and went away without trouble moreover the dogs were in fear of him. When I told her. Ladyship of this visitor she were greatly agitated and questioned me many times about him. She spent all the night talking with her son.

On the next morning which were the twentye first day of September they both did rise and dress as usual but would take no food and were in a rare state of excitement. She talked much of a King. They did pace about the rooms and ask me at every moment what time I thought it were and whether the sky be clear. At noon she called me to her and did embrace me and say Martha we are leaving here. She were with her son by the upstairs window and they both did step back and vanish into the air. Afterwards there were great cries from the people here, but not her Ladyship nor her son were never seen again at Hurnshaw House nor could any maner of searching find word of them or explain these things thereafter."

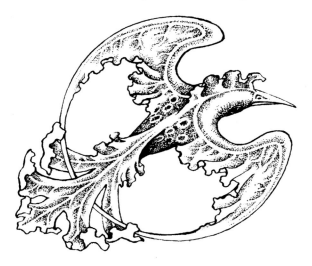

It is thought that Lady Elizabeth Hurnshaw originally brought eight notebooks and a folio with her from Amarantos. To date only three of the notebooks have been discovered in the library at Hurnshaw House. A member of the family* who was a keen amateur botanist during the Victorian era removed the other volumes, and as yet they have not come to light. Several paintings accredited to Elizabeth were recovered from an auction room sale in 1978, and it is hoped that others may be traced in time.

In the following pages we have presented as much of the available material as possible. It is hoped that readers will find this work as interesting and intriguing as we have.

* Footnote: — This same Hurnshaw studied the occult and believed that Elizabeth may well have been a 'witch'. For this reason he added to the family coat of arms the bust of a woman with a crescent moon on her brow (a symbol of the magic arts). Although this device was not accepted by the College of Arms, this version of the Hurnshaw arms has been reproduced here.

Una Woodruff, Mortitia Adams
and G. F. Hurnshaw 1981

26

The Flora of Amarantos

Elizabeth Hurnshaw
1687

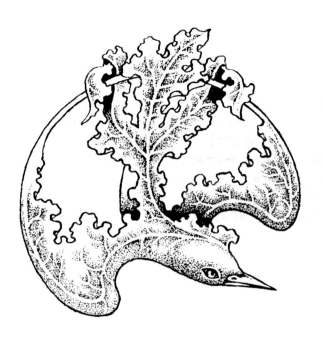

ΠΕΤΡΙΤΣΥΜΜΥΤΥΡΤΥΣ

Seeds

Stigma

Stamens

ΑΜℰΡℰVOS

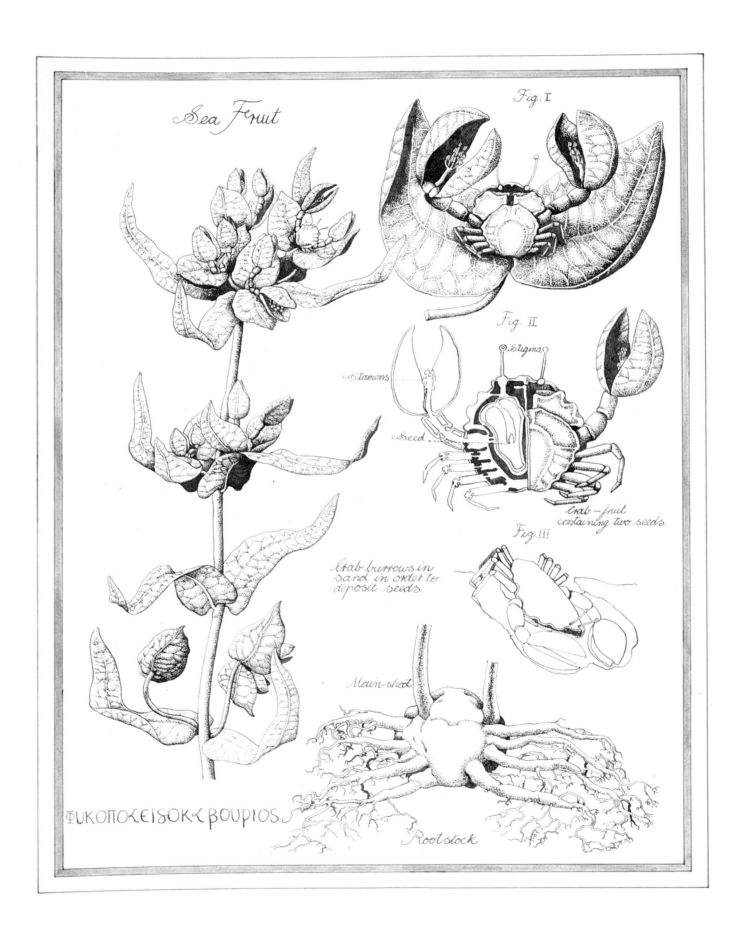

Sea Fruit

Fig. I

Fig. II

Stamens

Stigma

Seed

crab-fruit
containing two seeds.

Fig. III

crab burrows in
sand in order to
deposit seeds.

Main shoot

ΦΥΚΟΠΟΣΕΙΣΟΚΣΒΟΥΡΙΟΣ

Rootstock

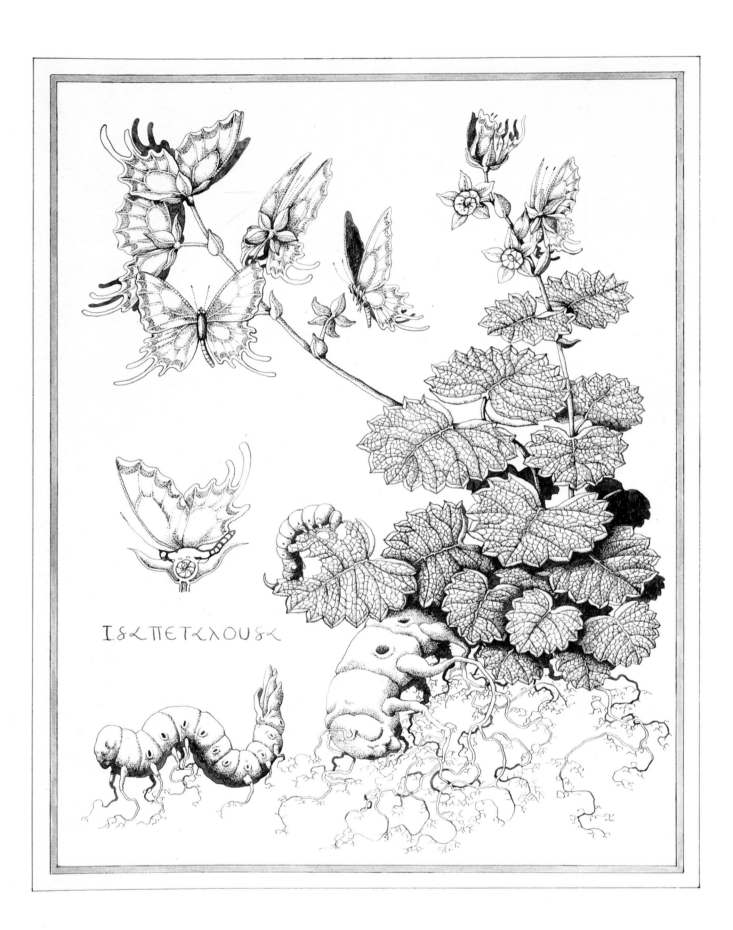

ISᗷΠETᗷλOUᗷᗷ

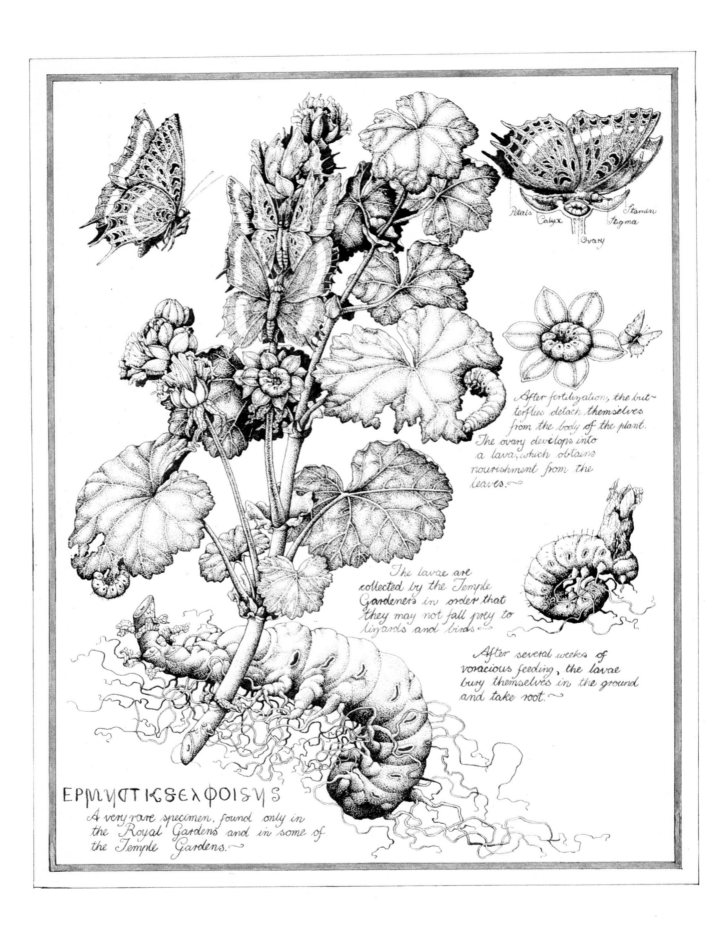

Petals Calyx Stamen
Ovary Stigma

After fertilization, the butterflies detach themselves
from the body of the plant.
The ovary develops into
a larva, which obtains
nourishment from the
leaves.

The larvae are
collected by the Temple
Gardeners in order that
they may not fall prey to
lizards and birds.

After several weeks of
voracious feeding, the larvae
bury themselves in the ground
and take root.

ΕΡΜΥΣΤΙΚΣΕΛΦΟΙΣΥS

A very rare specimen, found only in
the Royal Gardens and in some of
the Temple Gardens.

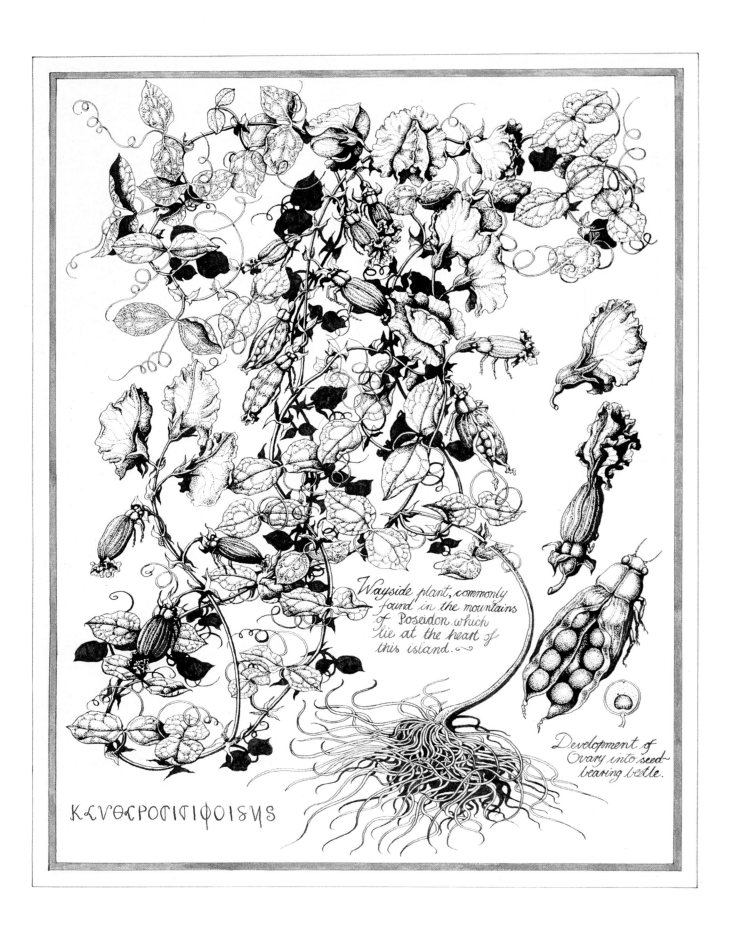

Wayside plant, commonly
found in the mountains
of Poseidon which
lie at the heart of
this island.

Development of
Ovary into seed
bearing betle.

Κᛌ Ⴍ ᛅ Ⴍ Ⴍ Ⴍ Ⴍ Ⴍ Ⴍ

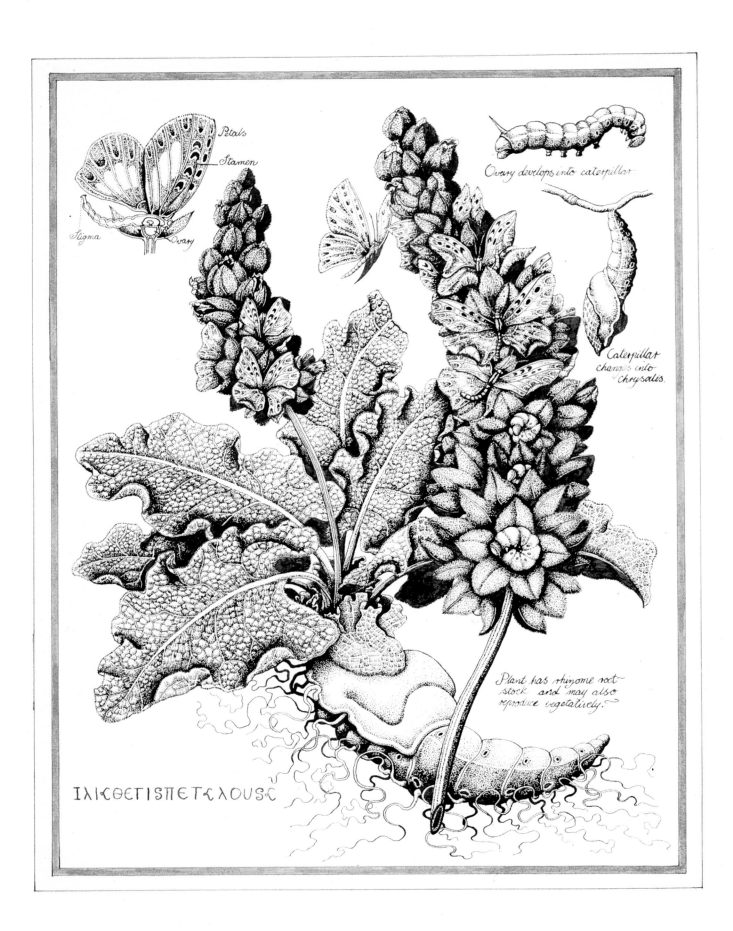

Petals

Stamen

Stigma

Ovary

Ovary develops into caterpillar

Caterpillar changes into chrysalis.

Plant has rhizome root-stock and may also reproduce vegetatively.

ΙλΙϹΘΕΤΙϽΠΕΤϛλΟUϽϹ

Male flower-head.

ΣΦΙΝξ~ΑΦΡΟSΙΤΥΡΜΥS

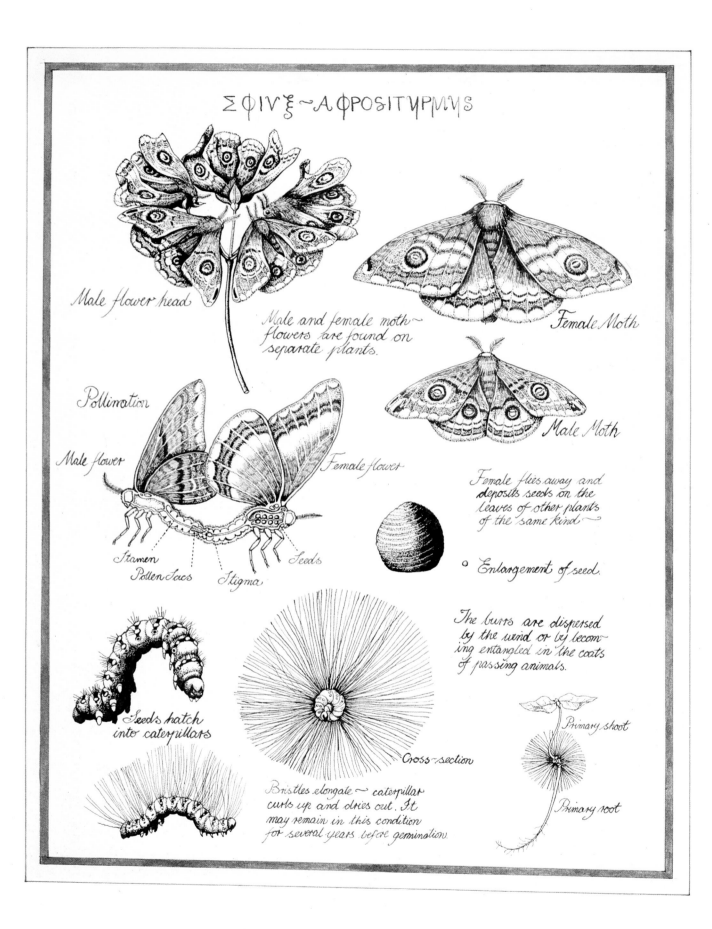

ΣΦΙΝΞ~ΑΦΡΟSΙΤΨΡΜΨS

Male flower head

Female Moth

Male and female moth~
flowers are found on
separate plants.

Pollination

Male Moth

Male flower

Female flower

Female flies away and
deposits seeds on the
leaves of other plants
of the same kind~

Stamen

Pollen Sacs

Stigma

Seeds

∘ Enlargement of seed.

The burrs are dispersed
by the wind or by becom-
ing entangled in the coats
of passing animals.

Seeds hatch
into caterpillars

Cross~section

Primary shoot

Bristles elongate ~ caterpillar
curls up and dries out. It
may remain in this condition
for several years before germination.

Primary root

47

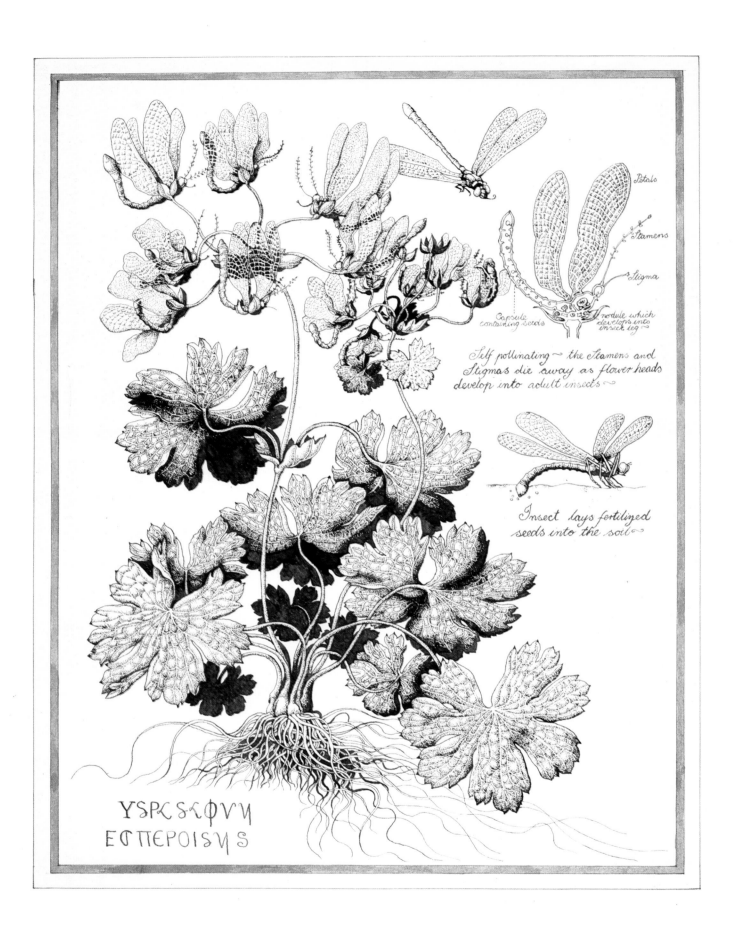

Petals

Stamens

Stigma

Capsule
containing Seeds

A nodule which
develops into
insect leg

*Self pollinating ~ the Stamens and
Stigmas die away as flower heads
develop into adult insects ~*

*Insect lays fertilized
seeds into the soil ~*

ΥSPΣSϞϕVꞀ
EϾΠEPOISꞀS

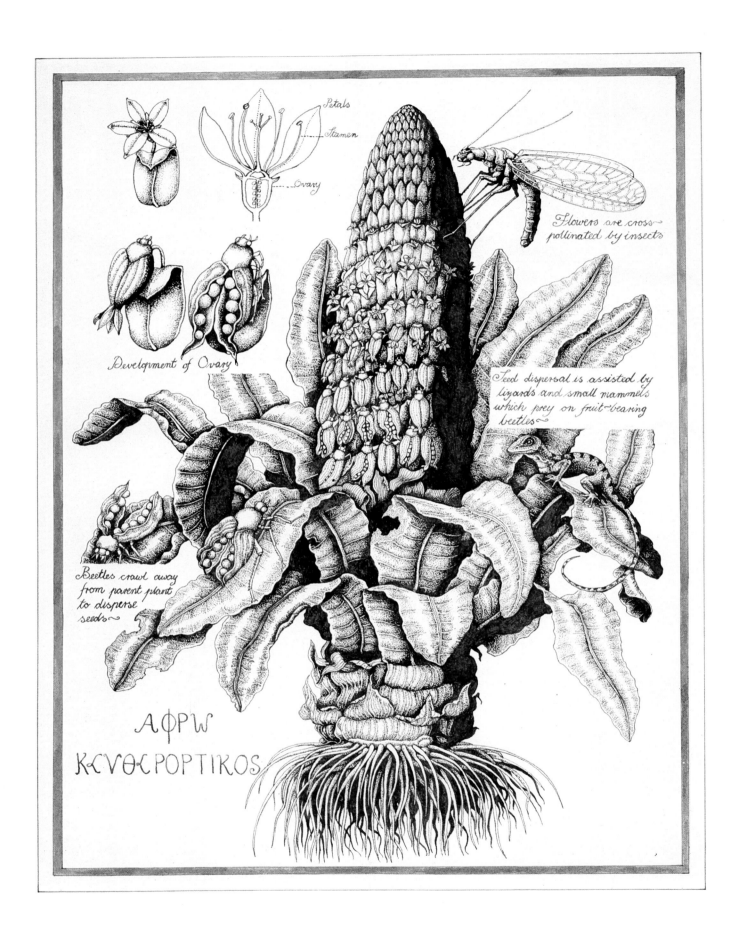

Petals

Stamen

Ovary

Flowers are cross-
pollinated by insects

Development of Ovary

Seed dispersal is assisted by
lizards and small mammals
which prey on fruit-bearing
beetles

Beetles crawl away
from parent plant
to disperse
seeds

ΑΦѠ
ΚϹѴΘϹΡΟΡΤΙΚΟS

The Dragon Vine

ΜΟΡΦΙⲤ~ΥⲤΡⲤΚⲤΛΥΨⲰ

Fig. I

Fig. II

Fig. III

Fig. IV

Elongated
Corolla

Section through flower.

Seed Pod

Stigma

Flowers are pollinated by
insects.

Stamens

The seeds are crushed, and the emerald-coloured juice
is made into a strong magic potion. Any who may
drink this are enabled to see the invisible
dragons who inhabit this land.

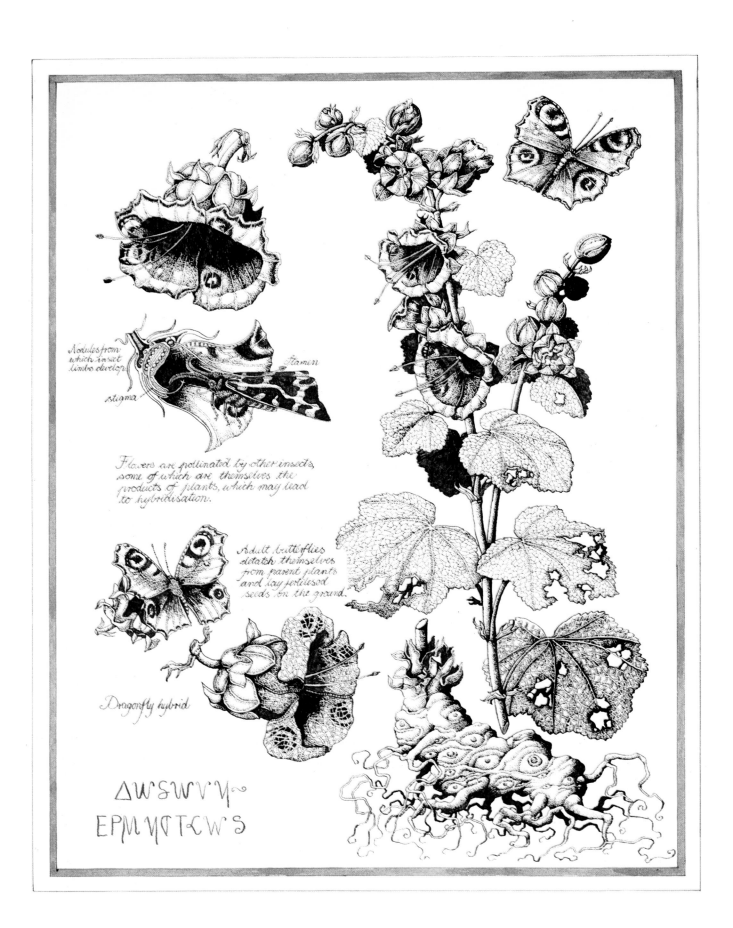

Nodules from which insect limbs develop

Stamen

stigma

Flowers are pollinated by other insects, some of which are themselves the products of plants, which may lead to hybridisation.

Adult butterflies detatch themselves from parent plants and lay fertilised seeds on the ground.

Dragonfly hybrid

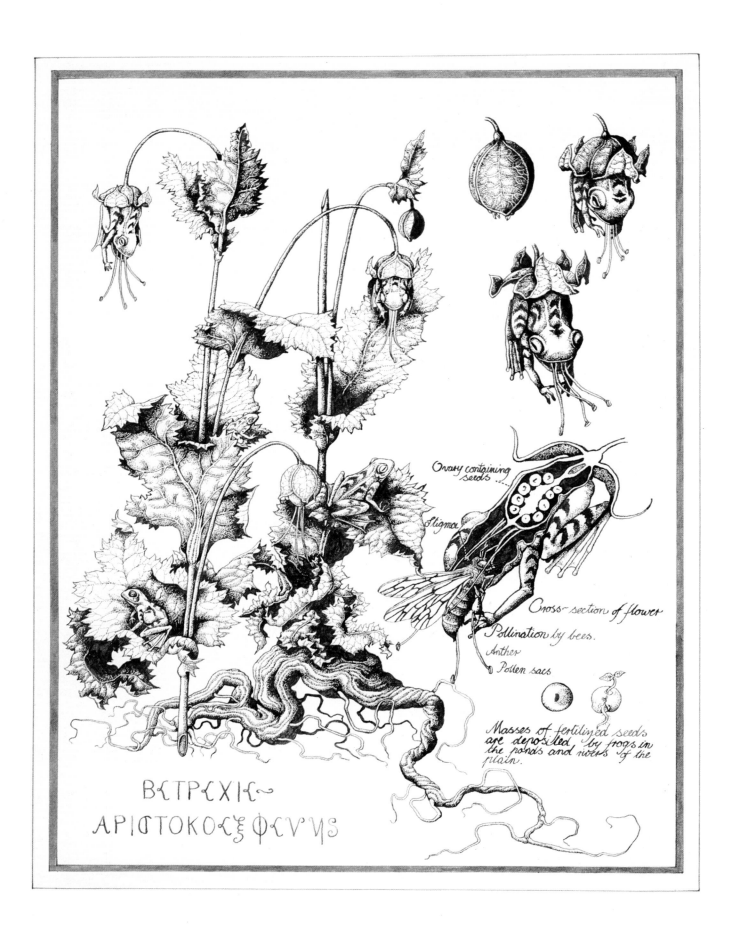

Ovary containing seeds

Stigma

Cross-section of flower

Pollination by bees.

Anther

Pollen sacs

Masses of fertilized seeds are deposited by frogs in the ponds and rivers of the plain.

ΒΕΤΡΕΧΙΕ

ΑΡΙΣΤΟΚΟΣΞΦΕΝΝS

AMPAVOS

Flora Nova Munde

Contents

Stinging Nettle

Desert Nettle

This plant has a most
vicious sting which may
be remedied by the timely
application of sap squeezed
from the roots.

The magical
flower which was gathered
from the sea in ancient
times by Gilgamesh, ancestor
of King Eunor.

The Flower of Immortality

Dandelion

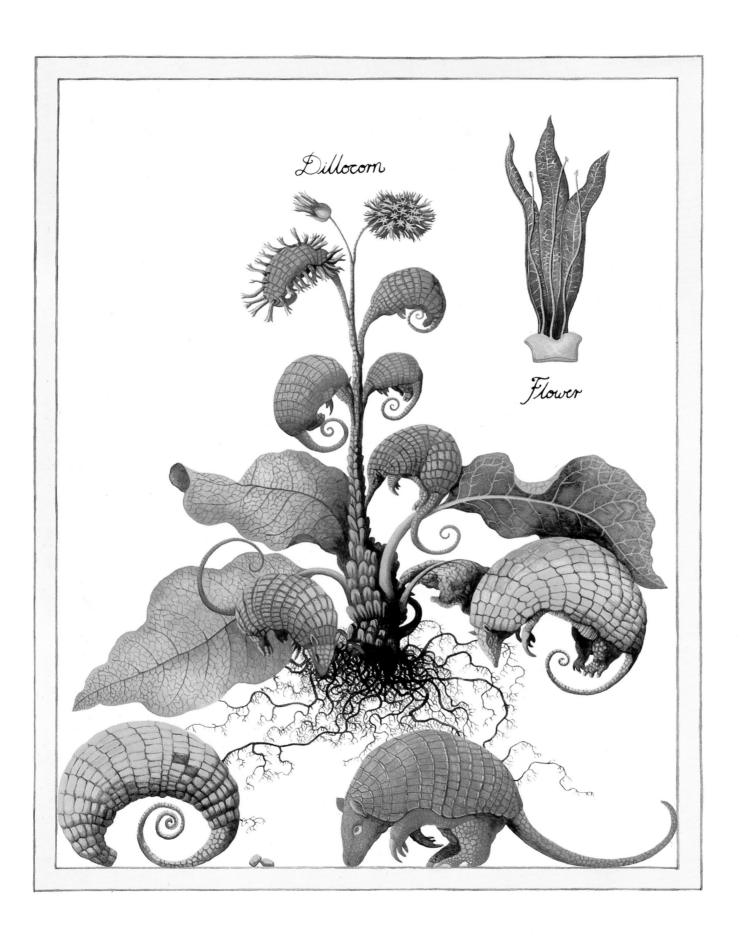

Dillocorn

Flower

The Barometz

The most useful plant which grows in this land is the Barometz or Vegetable Lamb. This fern has a root stem covered with white wool, which, in due course, develops into a complete and perfect sheep. On reaching maturity the Vegetable Lamb, which is rooted in the ground, stretches out its neck and feeds on the grasses growing in the vicinity.

The farmers grow many different varieties of these ferns which provide them with meat and wool. They are obliged to make their fields safe against wolves and foxes for whom the lambs are favourite prey.

Vegetable Mouse ~ a Baromety fern.

Rhizome stem

Tunnelwort ~ a Barometz fern
with a hairy rootstock which gives
rise to burrowing creatures which
are very similar to the common
Mole in their appearance and habits.

Hare's-foot Fern

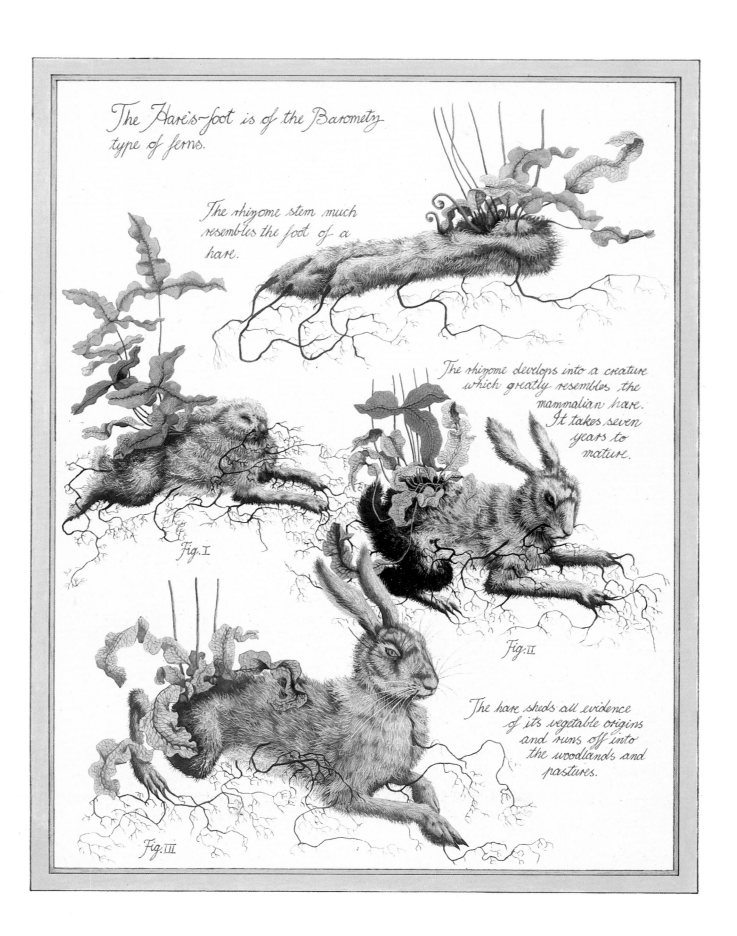

The Hare's-foot is of the Barometz type of ferns.

The rhizome stem much resembles the foot of a hare.

The rhizome develops into a creature which greatly resembles the mammalian hare. It takes seven years to mature.

Fig. I

Fig. II

The hare sheds all evidence of its vegetable origins and runs off into the woodlands and pastures.

Fig. III

81

When the number of hares becomes too great, the pesant farmers hunt them with dogs because of the destruction that they cause to the crops. After capture, the men are careful to destroy the creatures entirely, as any small part which may fall on the ground is likely to take root and develop into a new plant.

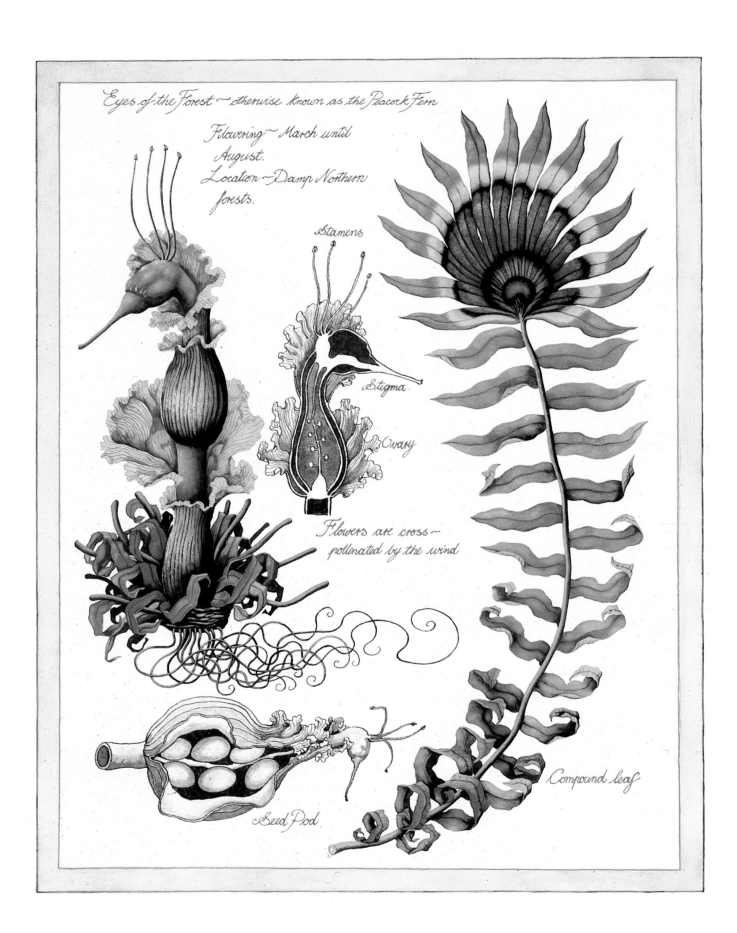

Eyes of the Forest ~ otherwise known as the Peacock Fern

Flowering ~ March until August.
Location ~ Damp Northern forests.

Stamens

Stigma

Ovary

Flowers are cross-pollinated by the wind

Seed Pod

Compound leaf

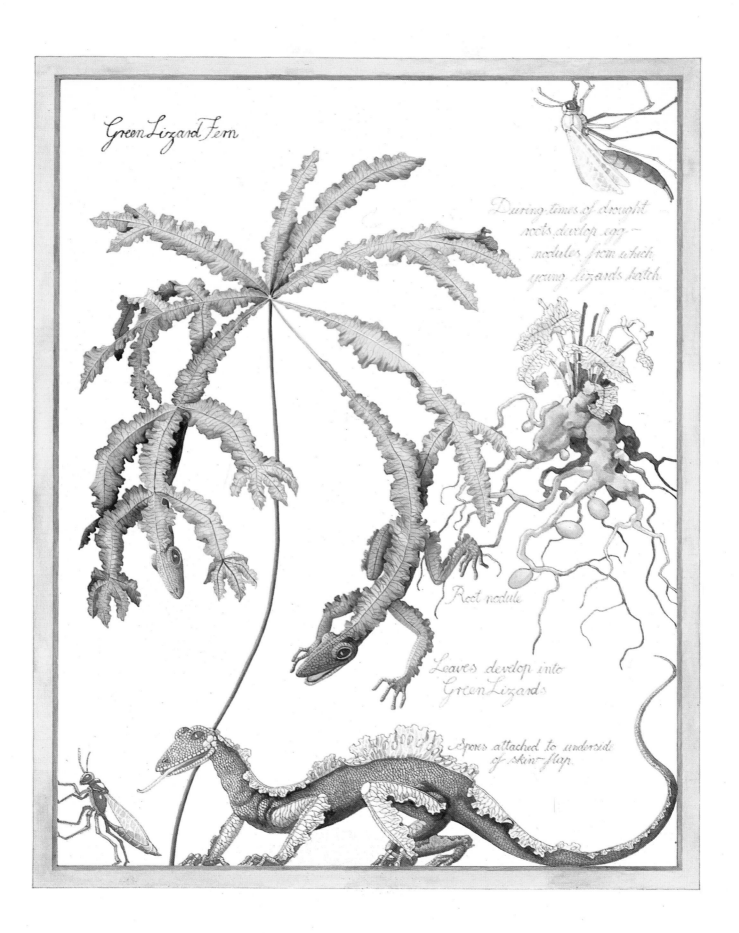

Green Lizard Fern

During times of drought
roots develop egg-
nodules from which
young lizards hatch.

Root nodule

Leaves develop into
Green Lizards

Spores attached to underside
of skin-flap.

89

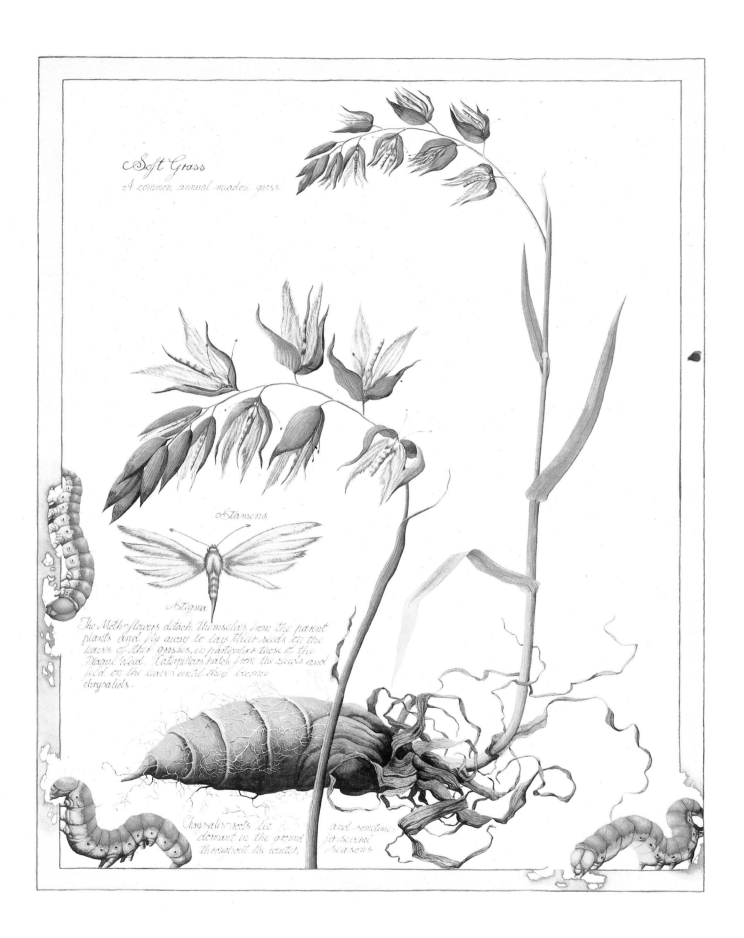

Soft Grass

A common annual meadow grass.

Stamens

Stigma

The Moth-flowers detach themselves from the parent plants and fly away to lay their seeds on the leaves of other grasses, in particular those of the Plague Weed. Caterpillars hatch from the seeds and feed on the leaves until they become chrysalids.

Chrysalis-roots lie dormant in the ground throughout the winter, and sometimes for several seasons.

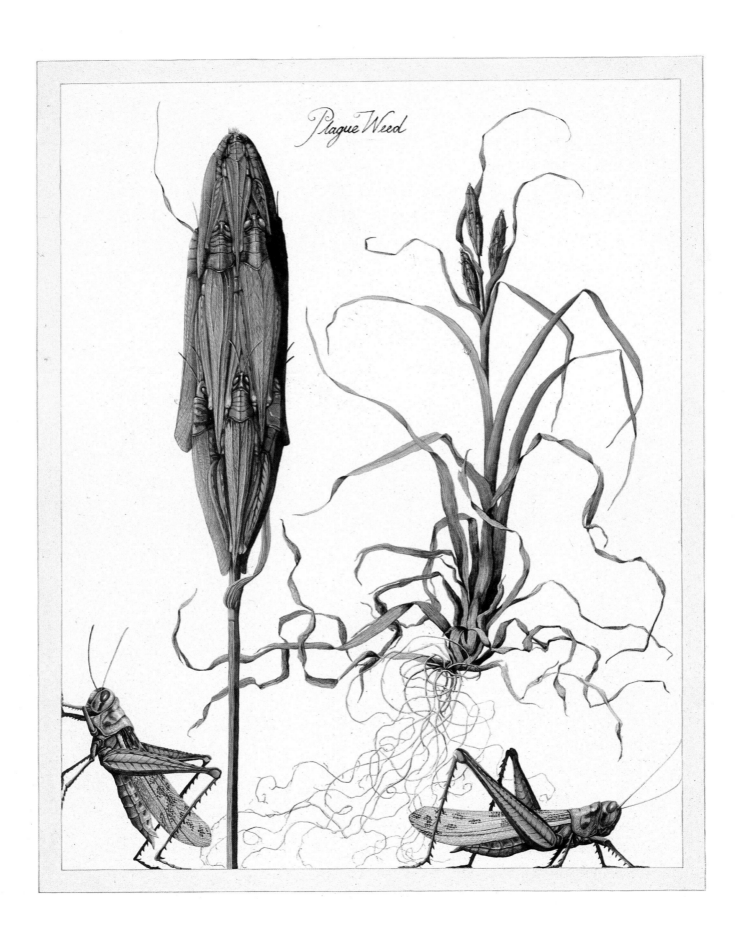

Plague Weed

Spider Grass

Stamen

Stigma   Seed pod

Pollen sacs

Stamen

Seed

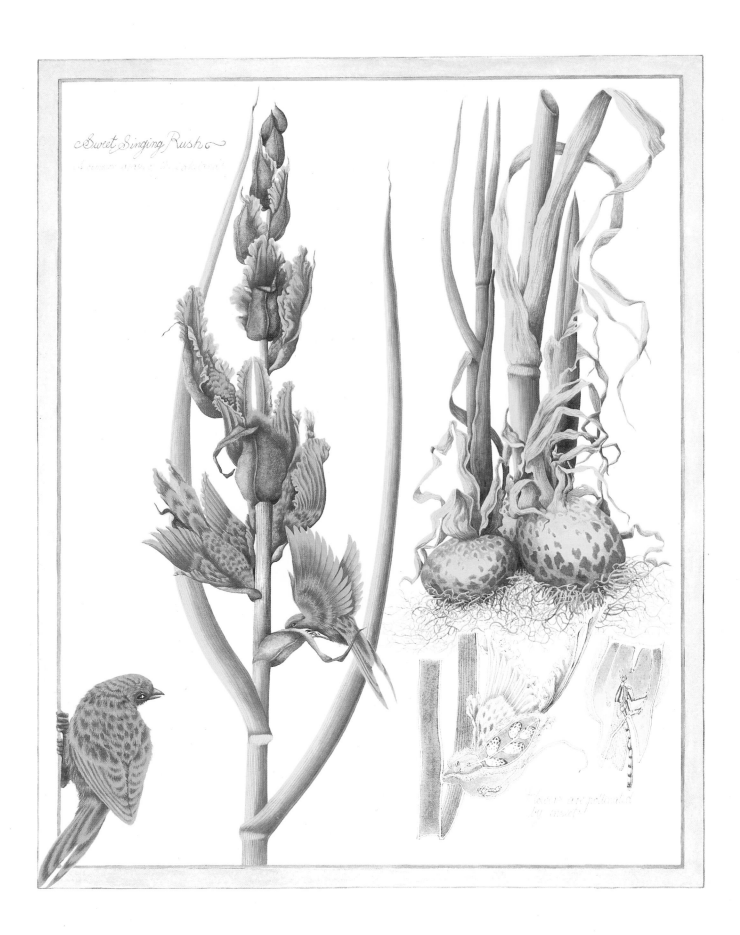

Sweet Singing Rush

98

Emerald Grass

Stamens

Seed Pod

Twilight or Maidenhair Grass

An uncommon parasitic grass which grows on the trunks of rotting trees.

The leaves are faintly luminous.

The roots often have the appearance of little manikins.

It is said that the manikins uproot themselves and may be seen singing and dancing together in the forests.

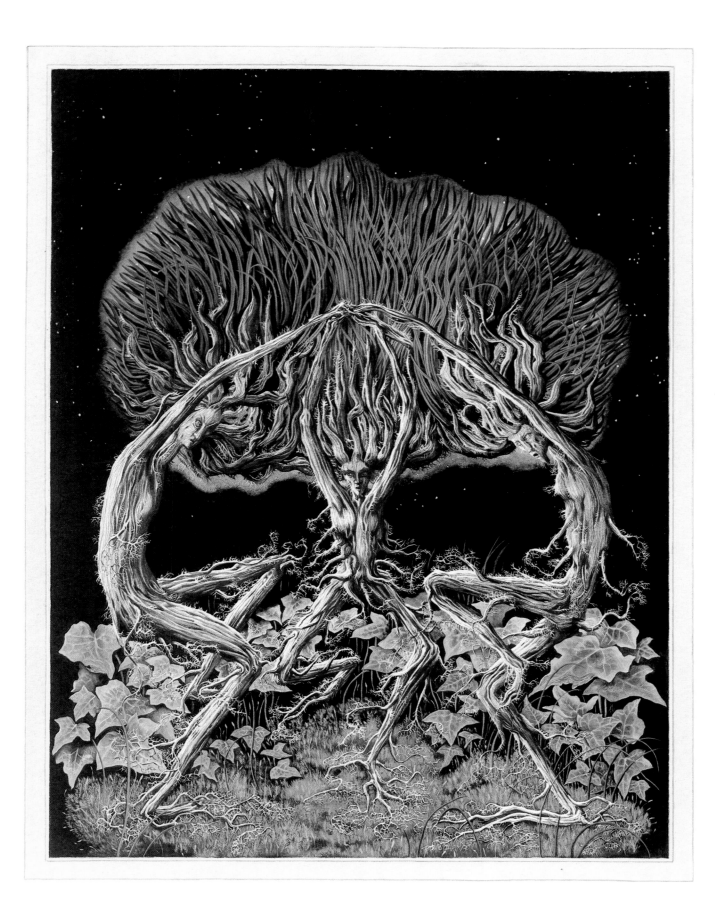

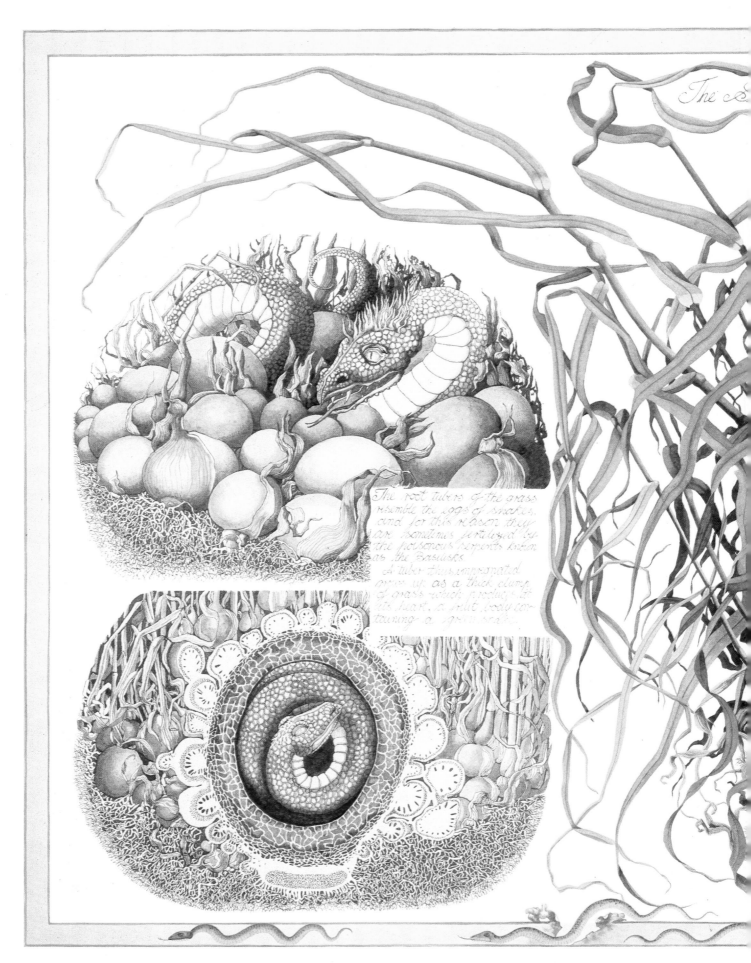

The root tubers of the grass resemble the eggs of snakes, and for this reason they are sometimes fertilized by the poisonous serpents known as the Basilisks.

A tuber thus impregnated grows up as a thick clump of grass which produces at its heart a fruit body containing a young snake.

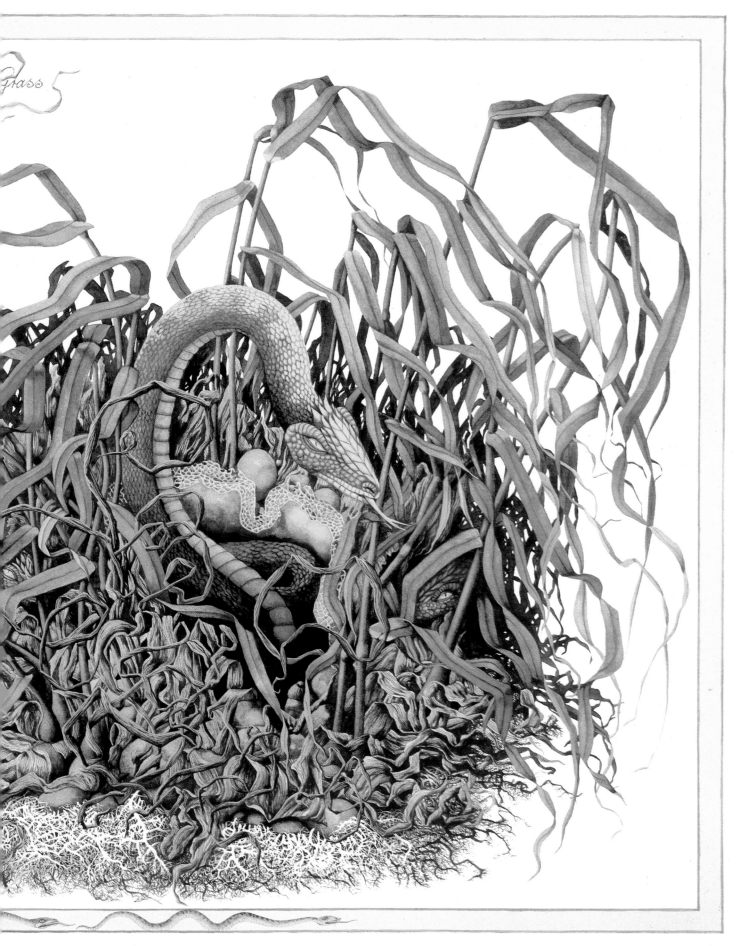

Grass 5

The Palace Gardens

ƐJꞍ
1695

Contents

The Bright~Stone

This stone pillar was placed by
the god Poseidon to mark the position
of the centre of the earth. It remained
in place even through the great dis-
aster which destroyed the island.

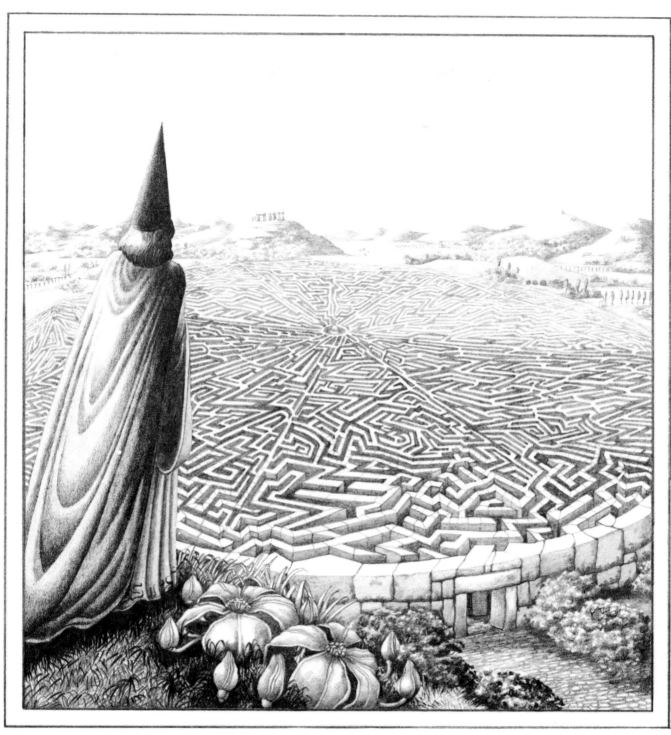

The Great Maze

Star~flower

Sun Dial

114

Moon Dial

Amarant

The everlasting flower which is traditionally given as a gift between lovers.

Leaf Boats
The leaves which fall from the
giant Tree are made into fishing
boats.

The Shrine of the Flower of Immortality
which lies at the centre of the Great
Maze.

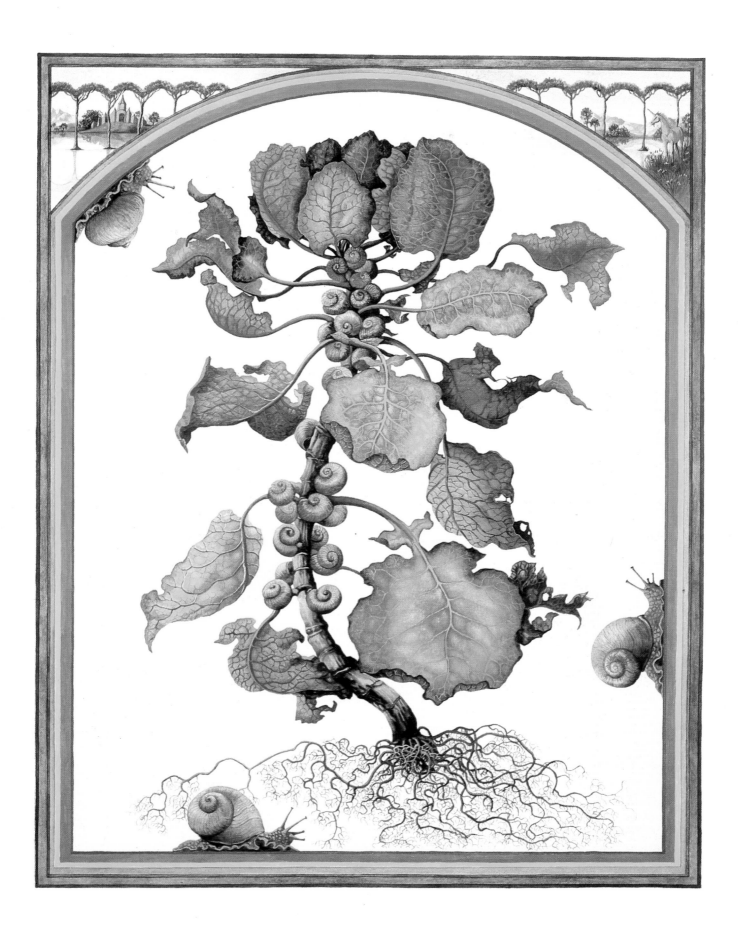

Lace~Web Spider

An uncommon insect which has the
habit of weaving into it's webs the
likenesses of surrounding leaves,
flowers and insects.

The Giant Tree
This tree, thought to be more
than twenty thousand years old, is
so vast that the people have built
a town amongst the branches.